I Get Up an...

by Selma Knight
Illustrated by Maria Perera

OXFORD
UNIVERSITY PRESS

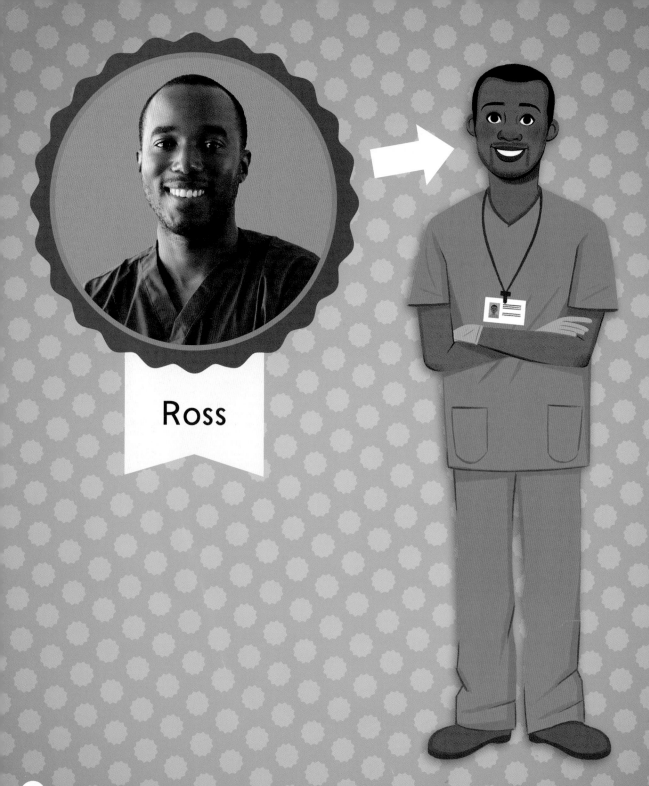

Ross

I fell off a big log.

4

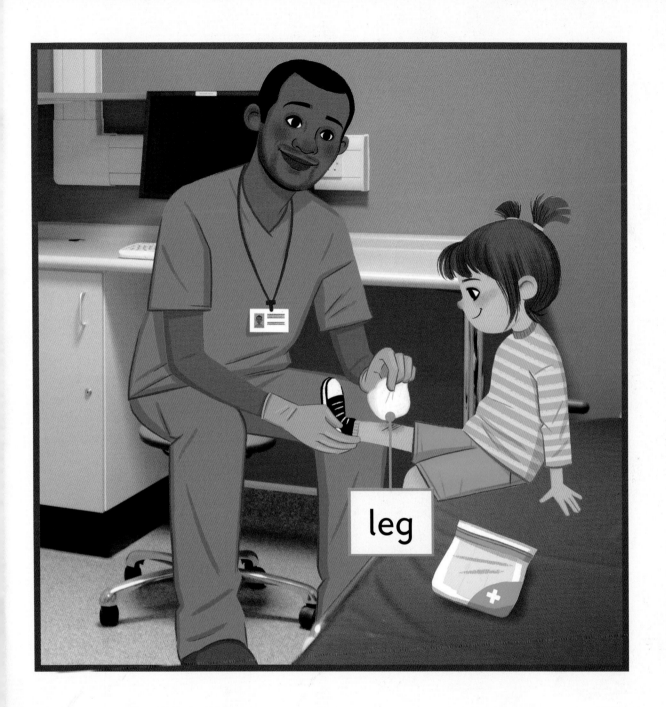

leg

Ross dabs the cut.

Ross gets the man back into bed.

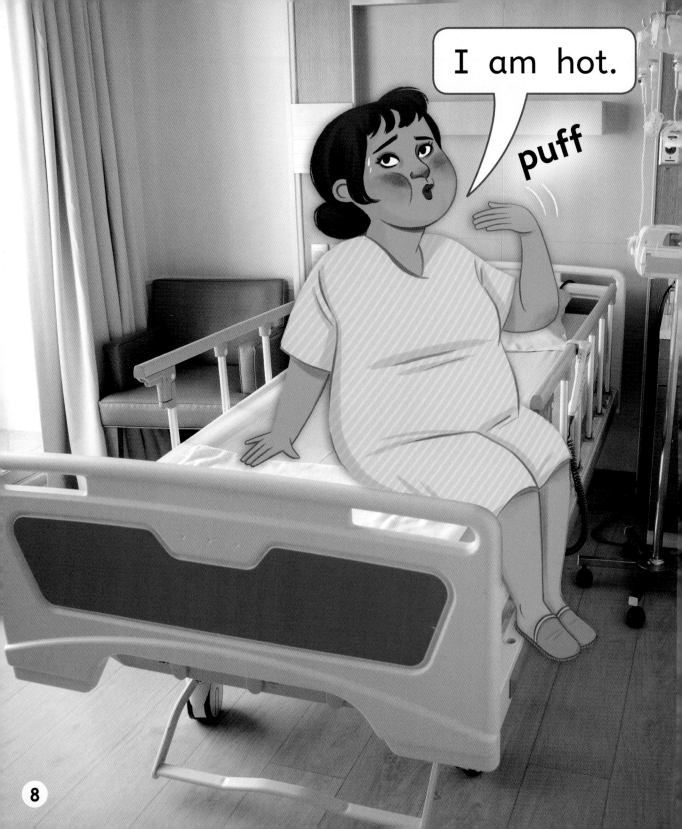

Ross gets a fan and a pill.

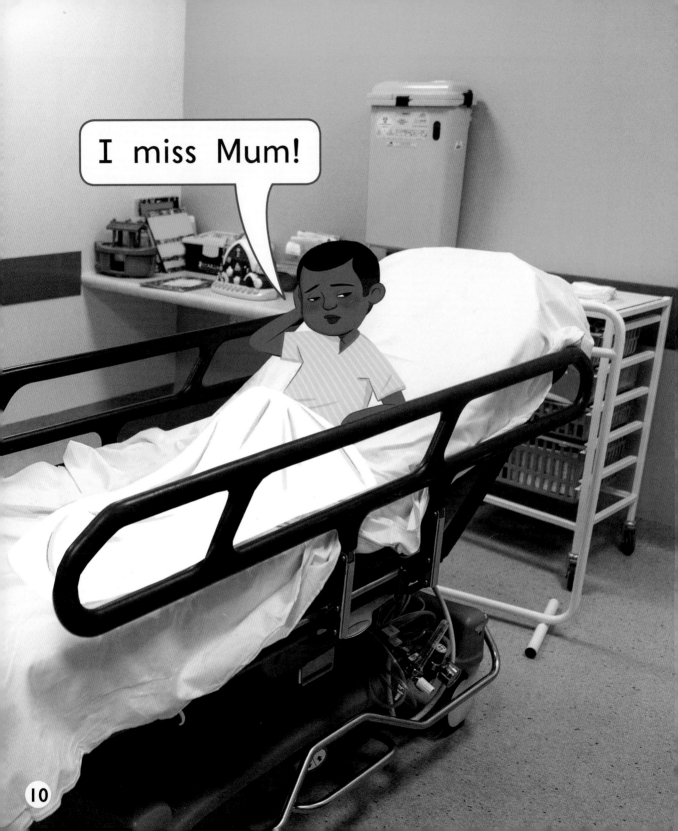

Ross gets Ted.

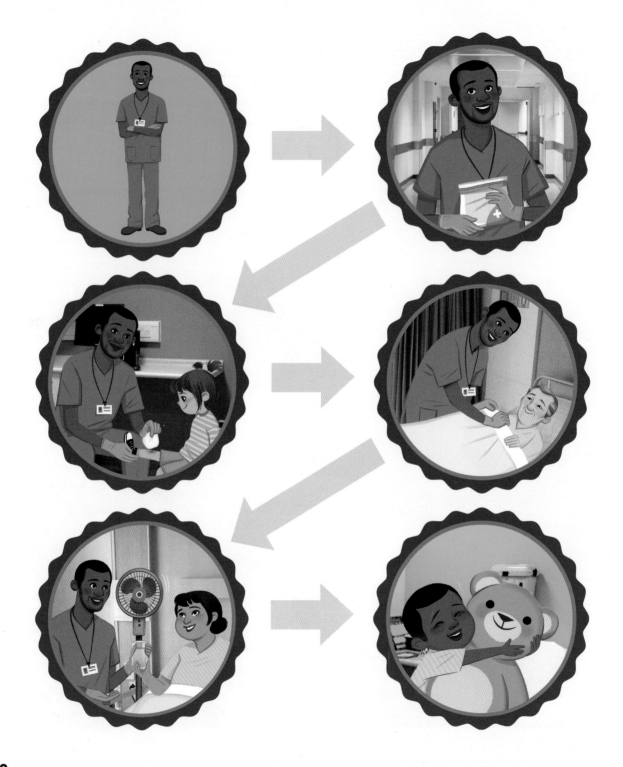